GEORGE BEST BELFAST CITY AIRPORT CELEBRATES 25 YEARS

Written by:
Editorial Solutions Ireland Limited
Researched by:
Ruth Kimbley
Designed by:
Leslie Stannage Design Limited
Published by:
TSO Ireland

Acknowledgements

GBBCA wishes to thank all of the staff for their kind contributions, experience, knowledge and interviews which helped in the production of this publication.
We wish in particular to acknowledge:
Guy Warner
Alan McKnight
Jack Woods
Stakeholder Communications
Shirley Appleton
Hammond W Coppinger
Northern Ireland Tourist Board
Hastings Hotels
Belfast Visitor and Convention Bureau
Thanks are also due to Flybe staff Andrea Hayes and Sara Randell Johnson and also to Sarah Weir at JPR for their contribution to the Flybe chapter.

Special thanks to the consortium of Sheelagh Hughes and Pauline Holland of Editorial Solutions, Roisin McAuley and Nicholas Scott of Leslie Stannage Design and Marie Maguire and her colleagues at TSO Ireland.

© George Best Belfast City Airport 2008 All rights reserved. No part of this publication may be reproduced, stored in a retrieval system, or transmitted in any form or by any means, electronic, mechanical, photocopying, recording or otherwise without the permission of the publisher. Applications for reproduction should be made in writing to The Stationery Office Ltd, St Crispins, Duke Street, Norwich NR3 1PD. The information contained in this publication is believed to be correct at the time of manufacture. Whilst care has been taken to ensure that the information is accurate, the publisher can accept no responsibility for any errors or omissions or for changes to the details given. The contributors assert their moral rights under the Copyright, Designs and Patents Act 1988, to be identified as the authors of this work. A CIP catalogue record for this book is available from the British Library. A Library of Congress CIP catalogue record has been applied for.

First published 2008

ISBN 978-0-337-09105-6

Printed in Northern Ireland by Graham & Heslip, Belfast, Co. Antrim

Contents

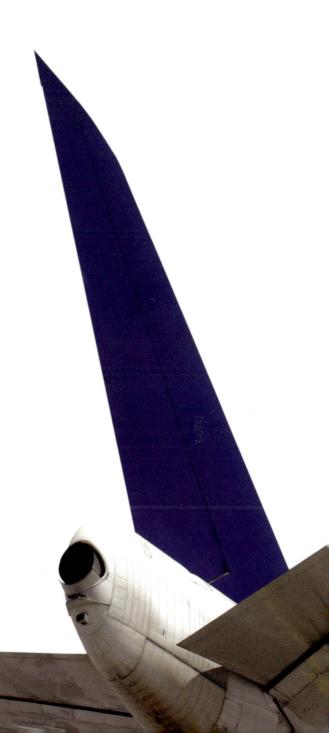

Foreword	5
Timeline - 1983 to 2008	6
Silver Threads - History	8
Silver Service - Staff	12
Silver Steel - Terminal	26
Silver Screen - VIPs	40
Silver Lining - Community	56
Sterling Silver - Tourism & the Economy	68
Silver Streak - Flybe	82
Golden Future	96
Facts & Figures	100

Foreword

The Rt Hon Peter D Robinson MP MLA
First Minister

As George Best Belfast City Airport reaches its quarter of a century milestone I am delighted to have the opportunity to reflect on the part the airport has played in Northern Ireland's past, its role in the present and the positive contribution it has to make to the future.

In some ways Northern Ireland and Belfast's economic history can be illustrated by the developments at Belfast City Airport. In our rich industrial past we know the airport was used for decades as a testing aerodrome for the aircraft industry. But as economic realities meant our city had become less reliant on manufacturing we have seen the airport rise to the challenge of providing a top-class business portal for Belfast.

As the MP for East Belfast for nearly 30 years I have watched as Belfast City Airport has woven itself into the fabric of this part of the city. It is vital for our local economic prosperity providing improved business links with the rest of the United Kingdom and Europe, not to mention the jobs delivered into the heart of the East Belfast community. I feel a sense of pride when I use it for both business and leisure as I remember what it has grown from. As an elected representative I am fully aware of the effort the airport and its management put in to their contribution to the local community.

The airport is part and parcel of East Belfast daily life. That is why I was delighted to be at the unveiling of the new name 'George Best - Belfast City Airport'. George was one of East Belfast's greatest icons, but more than that, he was also someone who brightened up the lives of everyone in Northern Ireland.

As First Minister one of my key responsibilities is to act as an ambassador for Northern Ireland. To deliver the prosperity that the people of Northern Ireland deserve, we must compete with other regions to persuade foreign investment that Northern Ireland is a good place to do business and that Belfast is a city on the up. Belfast City Airport makes that job easier. When people fly in they know that Belfast and Northern Ireland is open for business. The airport is the world's window to Belfast and Northern Ireland, the investment in the terminal and the infrastructure is clearly evident for visitors to see.

The recent purchase of the airport for more than £100m was one of the largest ever business deals Northern Ireland has ever seen. It displays a new confidence in our economy and our development as we face towards the future.

Congratulations to all at the airport on reaching this significant milestone.

Brian Ambrose
Chief Executive
for George Best Belfast City Airport

Belfast Harbour Airport opened its runway for commercial flights on the 7th February 1983.

Not many could have foreseen the airport's impressive rise over the next 25 years from humble beginnings in a Nissen hut to the multi-million pound, award-winning terminal now housing the airport's operations. A total of 83,000 passengers passed through the airport in our first year. By the end of 2008 we expect to welcome 2.7 million. This success can be attributed to the unique combination of determination and vision pursued by all of the airport's stakeholders.

In this our silver anniversary, it is appropriate to look back at developments at the airport, the staff that have helped make it such a success, and our continued involvement in the community, who I am repeatedly told are fiercely proud of the airport. This is a timely publication. Not only does it celebrate 25 years of growth and success, but it coincides with exciting new plans to develop the airport under our new owners ABN AMRO.

Northern Ireland and particularly Belfast is rapidly emerging as a tourist hot spot and our unrivalled location now acts not only as an important gateway for business but a positive first and last experience for the growing number of tourists. Additionally, the airport plays an important role in providing a direct service to the heart of the city, playing a pivotal role in the development of the Northern Ireland economy. As the fastest growing airport in the UK, we feel privileged that our continued development is good news for Belfast and the wider economy.

As a business we would like to thank all the passengers, business partners, local community and staff who have made the airport the success it is today.

I would also like to thank the members of the community, passengers and staff who have assisted in the compilation of this book. Special thanks must go to Ruth Kimbley from our marketing department who has worked tirelessly to assemble the publication you hold today.

I trust you will enjoy!

Timeline

The key milestones in the past 25 years

1983

The first official movements of Belfast Harbour Airport are on 7th February 1983. Spacegrand SGA 101 arrives at 08:25 from Blackpool, departing at 08:55 as the SGA 102 to the Isle of Man. Meanwhile, a Shorts 330 G-BGNA of Loganair arrives at 08:52 as the LC 433 from Glasgow. By strange coincidence, the inaugural flights of GBBCA mirror the first flights of Sydenham airport in 1938.

1988

The airport welcomes its one millionth passenger since 1983, one of a record total of 400,000 air travellers in this year. On 30th April the British Aerospace 146, dubbed the 'Whisper jet', is introduced and proves extremely popular with passengers, who enjoy the craft's superior speed and comfort. Des Kernaghan, the airport's first manager, retires.

1989

Parent company Shorts Brothers becomes part of Canadian aerospace giant Bombardier. Rapidly increasing passenger numbers prompt a major new investment programme.. 'Belfast Harbour Airport' is renamed 'Belfast City Airport'. Passenger numbers exceed the half million mark in-year for the first time.

1991

Two new routes to Cardiff and Leeds/Bradford are introduced. The Tall Ships visit the Port of Belfast. Pitts Special aerobatic aircraft treat the crowd to a spectacular air display which involves flying between the ship's masts. For the first year since its opening, passenger numbers do not grow, due to the effects of the recession and the Gulf war. The terminal's ground floor is turned into an Arrivals Building, and the boarding lounges and buffet area are refurbished.

1993

On 1st June the airport celebrates its 10th anniversary with a grand ball. The airport thanks its resident carriers: Jersey European, Loganair, Manx Airlines, Yorkshire European and Gillair. Jersey European launches its London Gatwick Service which fast becomes the airport's most popular route. The airport opens its first reservations office. A new Air Traffic Control Tower is constructed which incorporates a Fire Station and engineering workshops. A sponsored trip around the British Isles raises money for charity.

1994

Passenger numbers pass the five million mark since 1983. The in-year figure is over 1.25 million, representing a 44% increase over the past year. Air UK joins, bringing the Shorts Fokker 100 to the airport for the first time. Loganair passes its flights to sister company Manx Airlines. Jersey European adds a new route to London Stansted. Three of their jets now overnight in Belfast, which allows early morning business passengers to fly to Gatwick, Birmingham and Stansted.

1995

On 30th November US President Bill Clinton lands at GBBCA on his first presidential visit to Northern Ireland. The Presidential cavalcade and bodyguards line up on the runway as the US Navy and Marine Corps helicopters circulate the airport. After two successive years of impressive growth the airport passenger numbers level out at 1.28 million. GBBCA is now responsible for 44% of scheduled flights between Northern Ireland and the UK.

1997

On 1st July the Secretary of State for Northern Ireland, the Rt Hon Mo Mowlam, officially opens the new Arrivals building. The new building has been extended to reduce congestion and boasts an impressive viewing gallery for aviation enthusiasts. Heli-Trans Ltd, a civilian helicopter company, begins operations at the airport. At this point the airport's growth rate is twice the UK average. Four airlines operate 106 flights every week day to 20 destinations.

2001

On June 15th the new £21 million terminal at Belfast City Airport is unveiled at an official ceremony. First Minister for Northern Ireland, the Rt Hon David Trimble, formally opens the terminal. Also present are the Lord Mayor of Belfast, Minister Sammy Wilson MLA, and Vice President of Bombardier Ken Brundle. The new terminal has fixed ground power for ten aircraft.

2003

Ferrovial buys GBBCA from Bombardier for the sum of £35 million. In December the airport's two millionth passenger receives free flights from Flybe and a bottle of champagne from airport management. The passenger was among the 170,000 passengers who used the airport in December.

2006

On 22nd May Belfast City Airport is re-named George Best Belfast City Airport as a tribute to the local footballing legend. The decision was made in accordance with the wishes of the Northern Irish public. The unveiling of the new signage takes place on what would have been George's 60th birthday. The ceremony is attended by Best's family, friends and many famous faces from the sporting world including then Celtic manager Martin O'Neill and Northern Ireland goalkeeping legend Pat Jennings.

2007

On 6th February GBBCA receives the private sector Gold Award of Excellence at the Northern Ireland Quality Awards. In May, at the O2 Ability Awards, GBBCA is presented with the Environmental Accessibility and Customer Service Award. November is officially the busiest month in the history of the airport carrying more than 220,000 passengers. The airport caters for 2.2 million passengers this year.

2008

GBBCA is sold for almost four times what former owners Ferrovial bought it for in 2003. ABN AMRO Global Infrastructure Fund pays £132.5 million in September. Projected passenger numbers for 2008 are 2.6 million. Ryanair names GBBCA as its top airport for punctuality. GBBCA's main airline, Flybe, becomes Europe's largest regional airline following the acquisition of BA Connect, the regional airline of British Airways.

Silver Threads
The history of the airport

'Genuine beginnings begin within us, even when they are brought to our attention by external opportunities.' William Bridges

When George Best Belfast City Airport (GBBCA) opened for commercial activity with little fanfare in 1983 it was a bleak time for Northern Ireland. But things have changed. Now 25 years later, Belfast is a modern, vibrant city that combines bohemian qualities with a new affluence but remains a warm-hearted, idiosyncratic place. It is a source of pride to those who live here and of pleasure for those who visit. GBBCA is pleased to have contributed to that transformation.

The idea for a commercial airport at Sydenham really came about in 1971 when Captain F Hughes' BEA Trident 2, and two other planes, ran into difficulties flying over Belfast and were forced to make an emergency landing at Sydenham, then owned by Short Brothers and Harland Ltd. Impressed by the calm efficiency with which Ulster Radar and Shorts carried out the impromptu marshalling and refueling, the crew also noted that it took only 20 minutes from touchdown for passengers to reach the city centre. So why was this prime location not being used for commercial flights? In fact, it had been used for civilian flights as far back as 1938, but when World War II broke out it had been requisitioned by the Air Ministry as RAF Belfast.

Around the time Captain Hughes landed at Sydenham, Shorts were manufacturing the highly successful SD3 Commuter aircraft, which would potentially create efficiency and savings for airlines. Jersey European (as Flybe was known until 2002) was one of the first airlines to recognise the huge potential of low cost flying and of Sydenham's location and was one of two airlines that launched the airport's commercial activity in 1983. Short distance trips between Belfast and regional airports such as Glasgow and Blackpool attracted increasing numbers of passengers and the airport soon had to expand to accommodate them.

In 1989, a major capital investment in equipment and facilities was initiated and the airport's name was changed to the more representative Belfast City Airport. It was unrecognisable from what it had been just five years before. Passenger numbers soared, and by 1994 had passed the five million mark, increasing significantly year on year. The following year the airport, reflecting its new status, welcomed the President of America, Bill Clinton.

By 2001, when the attractive and modern £21 million terminal was formally opened by the First Minister for Northern Ireland, the Rt Hon David Trimble, the airport's success was assured. It was snapped up by the Spanish construction company, Ferrovial, in 2003 for the sum of £35 million.

The renaming of the airport to George Best Belfast City Airport in 2006 marked the next step in its remarkable journey, connecting it forever to the spirit of Belfast by honouring its favourite son.

GBBCA provides a gateway into and out of Belfast and helped open up Northern Ireland to business, industry and tourism. Its remarkable success mirrors the amazing regeneration of its city, and for both, the sky is very definitely the only limit.

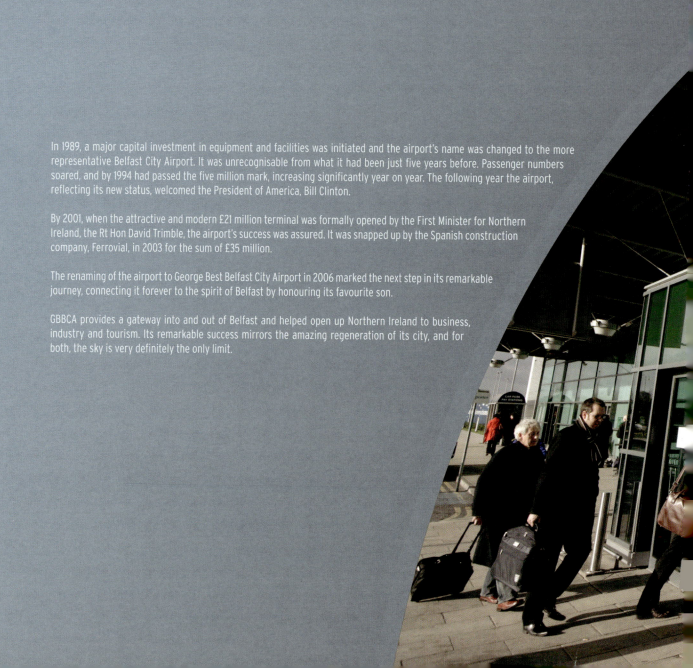

Silver Service

"Nice friendly staff – actually, it's a pleasure to use this airport. All airports should be like this." Mike Moore, passenger

The wind beneath the wings of GBBCA is certainly its staff. Over the years they have delivered a sterling service that has given the airport the enviable reputation of being friendly, efficient and welcoming.

Nowadays, surrounded by the latest technology, the airport's 1500 direct and indirect staff, whether customer facing or behind the scenes, ensure the effective running of the operation from check-in to take-off. But when the airport opened for business in 1983, things were just a bit different.

"We opened the airport equipped with a staff of four, a Nissen hut and a blank sheet of paper and pen," recalls the airport's first manager Des Kernaghan.

Lesser people might have panicked when faced with improvising with what, even in 1983, were very basic materials for a regional airport, but the staff's can-do attitude and competence ensured that everything ran to plan. The airport had, after all, been in operation since the 1930s, and however makeshift the materials, the confidence of management and staff never faltered.

Looking back now it's clear that all passengers flying out of GBBCA in those early days enjoyed the kind of service usually reserved for first-class passengers. The informality, freedom, and obliging friendliness of the staff rendered the experience closer to flying in a friend's private jet than the usual inconveniences and constraints sometimes associated with air travel. Delayed passengers could send out for fish and chips or whatever took their fancy. At check-in time, staff would even seek out passengers personally.

Staff expertise was not just confined to making the passengers' experience enjoyable and comfortable. Safety was, and is, always paramount, but until 1989, Air Traffic Control had no Instrument Landing System - the computerised system that provides precision guidance to an aircraft approaching the runway.

"We used to have to talk the plane down," recalls Alan Young, Manager of Air Traffic Services, "and the flight progress slips used to trace the plane's progress, were all handwritten."

Current Chief Executive of GBBCA, Brian Ambrose, like many of the airport's most senior staff, began his career in Shorts (now Bombardier). He remembers his first few days as being quite eventful. "I joined the airport staff in 1997 as Director of Operations. On my second day, the new Arrivals building opened. On the third day there was an aircraft overshoot on the runway. It was 'never a dull moment', and while many things about the airport have changed, that remains true. It's a great place to work."

High flyer: Dr Chris Lundy joined the airport in the late 80s moving from aircraft handling to statistical analysis and forecasting to Process Improvement Manager. His responsibilities as Environment Manager cover noise management, waste, energy, water and air quality – not only for the airport, but in relation to how that affects the operation of GBBCA partner companies working at the airport. "Today's challenge is planning an environmental management strategy that enables the growth of the business in a sustainable manner by minimizing the environmental impacts of the airport's operation."

Public Protection: Stephen Moreland, Head of Fire and Security, with Brian Ambrose and PSNI Inspector Alan McIlwaine in 2001. "The 9/11 tragedy changed airport security completely" Stephen recalls. "Security used to be carried out on a local scale, but now we receive regular reports on security from around the globe. Standards could not be higher."

Money talks: Raymond McNair, Director of Finance, talks business with Nuala Crolly in the Finance Department. Raymond has played a key role in the development of the business of the past 20 years. Nuala, who began as an Assistant Accountant in 1990, says: "My greatest achievement by far has been adapting to the sheer amount of change that has taken place at GBBCA. It's a rollercoaster!"

Duty calls: Louise McCutcheon, Airport Duty Manager, remembers a slower pace at the airport when she began on 28 May 1990. "With technology moving as fast as it has, life has changed dramatically and operational aspects are undoubtedly easier (though technology is not always as reliable as pen and paper!). But the airport has always maintained its welcoming family feel. The fact that typical days don't happen is one of the attractions of the job, although getting up at 4am is not!".

Marshalling the skies: Dr Chris Lundy Environment Manager, chats with Alan Young, Senior Air Traffic Controller. Alan began working at the airport in 1974, when the site operated as an RAF airfield owned by Shorts and the RAF. "Back then, I directed the test flying and training from an old World War II control tower on the airfield." The beauty of the job according to Alan, is that at the end of the shift you can just put your coat on and go home, leaving work at work. A luxury in this day and age!

What stress?: Martin Wallace, Air Traffic Controller, who has never missed a day's work in over 25 years. Martin attributes his record to the strong work ethic instilled by his parents. He gets up at 4.45am every morning to draw up progress reports on aircrafts and provides controllers with vital half-hour MET Office reports. Although air traffic control is considered to be a highly stressful job, Martin insists "I don't know what it's like to be stressed!"

Buddhist master: John Smyth, Security Manager with the Dalai Lama in 2002. John began at GBBCA in 1990. "The job description was a lot looser back then than it is now", he says. "Things like picking up litter and unblocking toilets mysteriously became security's job!"

At your service: Senior Firefighter Seamus MacMahon. Seamus was the first firefighter in Northern Ireland to receive an award for the top UK Leading FireFighter. He says "The best part of the job is the training. Often new recruits that come in are nervous, they think they won't make the grade. I train and guide them until they are fully competent and know that they can do it."

At the ready: Christine Richardson, the only female firefighter at GBBCA in 2008, loves the challenges of her job. "I was never anxious about working with 33 other male firefighters. I enjoy the banter, and I can give as good as I get!" On a daily basis, Christine's role involves inspecting all the appliances at the fire station including pump operations, water checks and breathing apparatus equipment, and of course responding to emergency situations.

Steeped in aviation: Brian Ambrose's career in aviation spans over 30 years. He began at the age of 16 as a Shorts' apprentice and gained expertise during his time there in every aspect of aviation including engineering, total quality, business and customer support. Brian became Director of Operations of the airport in 1997 and was made Chief Executive just a few years later.

Silver Steel

"This superb development for the new millennium will possess all the facilities of a world class regional airport and... will provide a suitably impressive gateway to the capital city of Belfast and to Northern Ireland."

James Stewart, Vice president of Bombardier Aerospace

Over 25 years GBBCA has undergone many reinventions, in name and in appearance. Today's modern terminal with its clean lines of silver steel, bears no resemblance to the small cluster of buildings that opened for business in 1983. Then, the airport terminal consisted of a Nissen army hut - harking back to when the RAF were stationed there during World War II.

The first passengers, mostly business people, crowded enthusiastically into the hut on 7th February 1983, enjoying the informality of the small, unorthodox terminal. The airport staff went out for tea and biscuits for everyone and then the Spacegrand SGA 102 plane took off for the airport's maiden flight to the Isle of Man, touching down to raucous cheers from passengers!

Very quickly, travellers began to appreciate the convenience offered by an airport in the heart of the city, and the volume of passengers rapidly grew. Even while the Nissen hut was being used by the first passengers, builders were hard at work converting what had been the RAF Officers' Mess into the new terminal, which opened in July of the same year. Around this time, GBBCA was known as Belfast Harbour Airport, its name since 1938. This name always had an uncomfortable resonance for pilots, who had a superstitious dislike of saying "we're coming into the Harbour"!

The chance to change the name and upgrade the image of the airport came in 1989 when Shorts was bought by Bombardier, heralding a new era. Bombardier announced a £1 million capital investment plan to create a more modern terminal and put the airport firmly on the national aviation map. The modernization plan delivered new instrument landing systems, surveillance radar equipment, a new aircraft parking apron, a fleet of fire and rescue vehicles, and a new air traffic control tower incorporating the fire station. The airport was completely transformed and renamed Belfast City Airport.

The airport's perfect location – mere minutes from the city, made it extremely attractive to those flying into Belfast. As its popularity increased it outgrew its facilities and in 1999 Bombardier announced a £21 million investment to create the modern terminal in use today.

There was, however, one more name-change in store for the terminal. When Belfast's favourite son, George Best, died in 2005, the unprecedented public outpouring of grief sparked a widespread debate on how best to honour his memory. After meeting with Best's family, the decision was made to rename the airport after one of Northern Ireland's leading lights. It became George Best Belfast City Airport on 22nd May, 2006, on what would have been George Best's 60th birthday.

In the beginning: Passengers make themselves comfortable in the airport's first terminal, the Nissen hut, as they wait for the inaugural flight on 7th February 1983. One woman was overheard exclaiming on entering the hut: "Oh this is so cosy!".

The way it was: The exterior of the purpose built security facility, pictured on 22nd June, 1983. Passengers passed through here before entering into the old terminal building. Shortly after this picture was taken a new terminal was opened, which had been the RAF officer's mess during World War II. This was the first of many developments and refurbishments that culminated in the modern terminal in use today.

Changing rooms: 1989 saw a major new investment programme for the airport that included a bright, welcoming and greatly expanded terminal. The airport's dramatic facelift coincided with a name change. 'Belfast Harbour Airport' became 'Belfast City Airport' to capitalise on the airport's convenient location.

Customer care: The new information centre, 1990. GBBCA has continually updated and improved customer provisions since opening in 1983. Its quest to provide a great airport experience for the passenger means it is responsive to changing passenger needs.

Sky at night: The characteristic blue and yellow triangle, pictured here, was the emblem of the airport from 1989 to 2006. When it was renamed as George Best Belfast City Airport it adopted the footballer's distinctive signature as the new branding. The airport's central location is also surprisingly picturesque, as it is situated by Belfast harbour with the Black Mountains in the background.

Stylish entrance: The new terminal was a far cry from the old Nissen hut! The terminal was opened by the Secretary of State, Mo Mowlam, in July 1997.

New millennium: An artist's impression of the current GBBCA terminal exterior. The new terminal has 2000 parking places, enclosed passenger walkways to the aircraft and improved access to the city. It opened in June 2001.

Fatherly pride: The late Dickie Best views his son's namesake at the official naming ceremony on 22nd May 2007, one year on from the day the airport was renamed. The ceremony was attended by Best's family, friends, and devoted fans. Brian Ambrose, GBBCA Chief Executive, stated: "This will act as a constant reminder of Belfast's favourite son."

Ready for anything: The new Air Traffic Control Tower, which incorporated a Fire Station and engineering workshops, was constructed in 1993. The new Visual Control room offered 360 degree viewing capability. The centre was 'home' to 46 staff members.

Blue skies: The stylish new silver and electric blue building heralds a new era of optimism for Northern Ireland. The futuristic architecture carries on Belfast's proud history of technological and engineering innovation.

Silver Screen

"There was David Soul tidying up the trolleys that had been abandoned. What a picture!" 'Airport Shirley' Appleton

GBBCA has seen its fair share of stars of the silver screen, stage and sports field. It has also welcomed many members of the royal family including the Queen and Princess Diana, and several heads of state.

Not all of them have pitched in with tidying the trolleys, but all have appreciated the friendly, relaxed atmosphere and good humour that inevitably bubbles up in staff when they are faced with a VIP.

This certainly is true of 'Airport Shirley', as christened by John Daly on his BBC Radio Ulster show. Shirley worked at the airport's World News and Deli Sandwich Bar for five years. She met hundreds of celebrities "almost on a daily basis", and kept a record of her time there, becoming something of a celebrity herself along the way. Here are some of her memories...

"Good old Eamon (Holmes), what a character! I would always have a wee chat to him. He was in one day and I missed him so he told my colleague, Donna, he would send me a message on GMTV. A few days later there he is sitting on the GMTV sofa and he said my name, 'Shirley Appleton,' and goes on to tell Fiona about this mad woman who tortures him (in a nice way) every time he is at Belfast City Airport. I was well chuffed - fame at last! - and to put the icing on the cake I had a hospital appointment that morning and the doctor asked was I the 'Shirley Appleton' who was mentioned that morning on GMTV!"

Shirley also remembers Northern Ireland's favourite VIP, George Best, passing through the airport that would become his namesake. "I was lucky enough to meet George twice - I kind of pulled rank on Johnny, another member of staff, so that I could serve George and Alex. They were such a lovely couple. Later, when George was in hospital, I met Calum and told him we were all thinking and praying for his dad. He seemed genuinely grateful that someone had spoken to him about his dad."

Other celebrities that Shirley met as they passed through the terminal included Roger Daltry, Colin Bateman, David Soul ("I actually went bright red and tongue tied!"), Darius, David Bellamy, Marie Jones, Tara Palmer Tompkinson, Norman Wisdom, Westlife, Jimmy Nesbitt, Eddie Izzard, Girls Aloud, Dr Hooke, Keith Chegwin, Take That, Graeme Norton and James Bond himself, Roger Moore.

Chief Executive, Brian Ambrose, believes that characters like Shirley are what imbue GBBCA with its unique charm. "For many VIPs, the airport is their first impression of Northern Ireland. The first thing they see is the terminal and the first people they speak to are the staff. So this good humoured repartee is more significant than it might seem: it welcomes visitors to Northern Ireland with genuine warmth."

Royal visit: Mark Beattie, Operations Director, welcomes HRH Queen Elizabeth to GBBCA. The Queen was on an official visit to Northern Ireland to mark the disbandment of the Royal Irish Regiment.

Racing star: Matthew Allison of Airside Standards with Lewis Hamilton in January 2008. "It was a miserable day and I was absolutely soaked but he was happy to pose for photographs… I wished him all the best for the coming season and we shook hands…then he was on his way back to McLaren to sign his £10 million contract!" Lewis was in Belfast for Bombardier's centenary celebration, as Brand Ambassador for their Learjet business jets.

Travellin' light: 'Airport' Shirley adds Sir Cliff Richard to the long list of celebrities she has met when he flew into GBBCA in 2004. Shirley met hundreds of famous people when she worked in the airport's World News outlet.

At ease: The late Diana, Princess of Wales, chats with Hammond Coppinger, Security Director for Bombardier and the Lord Lieutenant, on a royal visit to Northern Ireland in December, 1994.

Warm welcome: Prince Philip pictured arriving at the airport on a royal visit in August, 1994, with Hammond Coppinger, Security Director for Bombardier.

Best buddies: Calum Best pictured here in September 2000 was a regular visitor to the deli bar where 'Airport Shirley' worked. She also met his father, George Best, twice and got his autograph, now a treasured possession.

Royal handshake: Prince Andrew is welcomed at GBBCA in 1995. The Prince was on an official visit to Northern Ireland to mark the disbandment of the Royal Irish Regiment.

"What about you!": Prince Charles is greeted by Brian Ambrose and Ian Pearson MP as he touches down for a royal visit, 7 July 1994.

"And what do you do?": Hammond Coppinger, Security Director for Bombardier greets the Duchess of Kent in December, 1993, on her arrival at the airport.

Street credibility: Celebrities who passed through the airport included Coronation Street stars, Bill Tarmey, who plays Jack Duckworth and Samia Smith, better known as the street's hairdresser, Maria Sutherland, seen with GBBCA's Market Development Manager, Lynda McCorry.

Silver Lining

"I want to thank you for all the work and commitment you have shown to the children. I am aware how much they have appreciated your work in Time to Read and the difference you have made with the children you have been supporting."

Graeme McKimm, Education Manager, Business in the Community

It would be fair to say that not everyone welcomed the idea of an airport in the heart of East Belfast. But even the most ardent opposers recognise the enormous contribution that GBBCA has made to the local community.

Over 25 years the airport has sought to give more than a little back to the community, with countless activities to raise money for Northern Irish charities and, in particular, a range of initiatives to help young people and local schools. With everything from fashion shows to training initiatives, guided tours, Christmas choirs and Fire and Rescue Service demonstrations, the airport's staff and management have demonstrated boundless enthusiasm and tireless commitment to building strong, positive ties with the community.

"Over the years the efforts of airport staff together with the generosity of the public have resulted in tens of thousands of pounds being raised to help improve the quality of local children's lives," says Michelle Hatfield, HR Manager.

Some of the charities that have benefitted from these efforts include the Royal Belfast Hospital for Sick Children, Marie Curie and the Northern Ireland Cancer Fund for Children (NICFC). Senior and Corporate Fundraiser of NICFC Joanne Steele says: "Financial security is one of the most immediate pressures placed on a family when a child is diagnosed with cancer. I would like to thank the City Airport and their wonderful staff for all their hard work in helping to raise money for us."

Each year GBBCA forms a partnership with a new charity, extending its reach and support for local people across Belfast and beyond.

Listening is a major part of the airport's approach to good community relations. In 1993, it established the first airport consultative committee in Northern Ireland. The Forum has an independent Chairman and representatives from local authorities, residents groups, the NI General Consumer Council, the Department for Regional Development, airlines and other groups.

Meeting with airport management on a regular basis, the Forum discusses all issues relating to the development and operation of the airport.

As well as continually monitoring noise complaints and airport performance, the Forum from time to time takes a more detailed look at issues of interest and concern.

One of these concerns is inevitably the effect of the airport on the environment. "We're constantly monitoring our impact on the environment and looking for ways to improve," says Dr Chris Lundy, Environmental Manager. "We have a programme of sustainable development, and are committed to achieving a balance between the social and economic benefits of the airport's growth, and the environment."

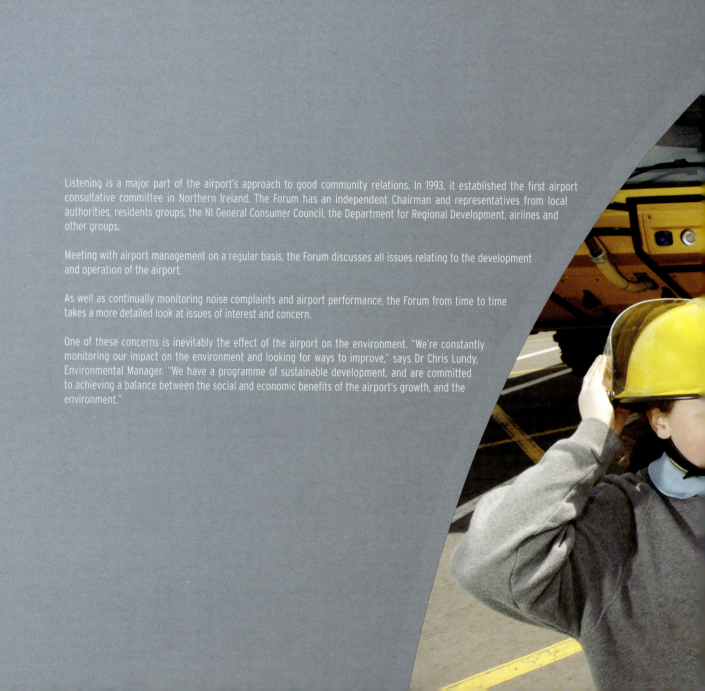

On tour: Representatives of east Belfast's Palmerston Residents Association get a tour of GBBCA in August 2008, to see at first hand how all aspects of the airport operate, from air traffic control to the fire service. Tours like this are all part of GBBCA's ongoing effort to stay in close communication with residents and listen to their concerns. Pictured are Sam Budde, Terry Hoey, and Raymond Hooke, Customer Services Manager, GBBCA.

Prize winner: Brian Ambrose, Chief Executive of GBBCA is named as the Prince of Wales Ambassador for Corporate Responsibility in Northern Ireland 2008. Mr Ambrose has carried out extensive work for charity and demonstrated his commitment to diversity within the workforce by his involvement with Business in the Community's Opportunity Now campaign. He is pictured with Michael Ryan, Chairman of Business in the Community.

Smiles all round: Michelle Hatfield, Human Resources Manager at GBBCA presents £20,000 to Joanne Steel (left), Senior and Corporate Fundraiser at the Northern Ireland Cancer Fund for Children. The airport raised over £10,000 in 2008 from a variety of events, and then matched what it had raised, bringing the total donation to £20,000.

Where's my present?: Santa makes an entrance by helicopter in 1993, on what must have been the reindeers' day off. Each year he arrived at GBBCA in a different way, adding an element of surprise to the Christmas festivities.

Getting down to business: The Forum has representatives from community groups, business organisations, central and local government, resident airlines and the General Consumer Council for Northern Ireland. It meets regularly to discuss matters such as airport operations, noise management and future development plans. The Forum's Sub Committees hold further detailed discussions.

Singing Santas: Redburn Primary School Christmas Choir with ITV presenter Julian Simmons, switching on the Christmas lights in 2006. Standing behind the children are Julie Campbell, Marie Curie, Raymond McNair, Finance Director GBBCA, and Joanne Deighan, Commercial Manager, GBBCA. The airport was transformed into a festive circus, with conjurors and acrobats from the local circus school performing to raise money for Marie Curie Cancer Care. The airport raised funds to provide 400 hours of specialist nursing care.

Festive cheer: The pupils of Hunter House College sing carols at Christmas 2006 in the airport to raise money for Marie Curie.

Riding high: Graham Bennison, Alistair Carmichael, Paul Noble and Colin Surgeoner from the Fire Station, pictured with representatives from Christian Aid and Habitat for Humanity.

Walking on the runway: Patrick Hughes, Station Commander at GBBCA, takes Mersey Street Primary School pupils for a guided tour around the airport. The entire school was there for the day to witness first-hand how an airport works. Lucky P5, P6 and P7 pupils got to go 'airside' and experience the sights and sounds of the airway first-hand, while younger pupils were treated to a live puppet show.

Tsunami NI appeal: Lord Rana of Andras House Ltd accepts a donation of £10,000 in February 2005 from Brian Ambrose Chief Executive, GBBCA for his tsunami appeal. This was an unprecedented donation from the GBBCA's charity fund in response to the tragic natural disaster in the Indian Ocean.

Sterling Silver

"Through GBBCA's location in the very heart of the city, their forward thinking and friendly atmosphere that encapsulates everything about Belfast, we have witnessed a growth in visitors to Northern Ireland and we have improved access to markets for export companies, both important contributors to economic success." Ann McGregor, CEO of NI Chamber of Commerce

When the first commercial flight took off from the then Harbour Airport in February 1983 against a background of global recession, local economic gloom and political tensions, it was a vote of confidence in the future of Northern Ireland's economy and its tourism potential.

And as the 80s progressed this confidence was vindicated. By the end of the decade, figures recorded by the Northern Ireland Tourist Board (NITB) showed a substantial increase in visitor numbers, with over one million in 1989, who generated £136 million for the economy and 10,000 jobs within the tourism sector.

Central to this growth was the improved air access to the region and Belfast City Airport's significant role as a commuter airport.

As the Belfast Telegraph reported on December 11th, 1989: "Growth at Belfast City Airport is described as 'phenomenal'." This was almost certainly due to business people who found the convenience of the airport a real boon to doing business in Great Britain.

Local businessman, John McGrann, recalls: "As the City Airport introduced more domestic routes, it made doing business on the mainland so much easier. It became possible to travel directly to places like Leeds, Bristol and Southampton, which previously had required long onward journeys."

As more airlines began to operate out of the airport, the business travellers were joined by increasing numbers of tourists. Manx Airlines were one of the first to introduce charter flights for holidaymakers from the City Airport and they were quickly joined by Jersey European Airways offering low cost flights to popular holiday destinations such as Blackpool and the Isle of Man.

Throughout the 90s and this current decade the regeneration of Northern Ireland and Belfast continued to draw increased numbers of tourists, while Belfast's development as a major conference centre consolidated its position as a serious business destination. The City Airport firmly established itself as the gateway to Belfast and expanded to reflect its growing success.

Sinead Maguire, Communications Officer, NITB, says: "George Best Belfast City Airport has helped to encourage people to travel to Northern Ireland, providing direct air flight routes from across Great Britain and Europe and ensuring a warm welcome to all who arrive. Increasing visitors to Northern Ireland means a boost to our economy with the revenue generated by tourism almost doubling since the mid 90s."

Today, in 2008, GBBCA is a major regional airport handling over 2.5 million passengers each year and flying to 21 UK airports and 6 airports abroad. The passengers that it welcomes to Northern Ireland, whether business people or tourists, bring spending power that is boosting the local economy by millions of pounds each year.

Message of hope: Tens of thousands of people turned out to greet President Clinton's first visit to Northern Ireland in November 1995, 15 months after the IRA announced its first ceasefire. President Clinton was the first US President to take an interest in Northern Irish politics and his influence was a turning point in the peace process. President Clinton flew into GBBCA complete with an escort of US navy and US Marine Corps helicopters.

First for punctuality: In September 2008 Ryanair, Europe's largest low fares airline, named GBBCA as its most punctual base. Between November 2007 and August 2008, 94% of Ryanair flights at Belfast Airport were on time. Punctuality is essential for GBBCA passengers whether leisure or business travellers.

Don't look down!: The Carrick-a-Rede Rope Bridge leads to an island which offers stunning views of Scotland and Rathlin, not to mention unique geology, flora and fauna for wildlife enthusiasts. The walk to the bridge has breathtaking coastal views for those that feel the 23 metre drop too daunting! Many tourists arriving at GBBCA continue their journeys up the famous Antrim coast road which encompasses areas of outstanding natural beauty, including the site of the rope bridge.

Natural wonder: The Giant's Causeway continues to attract hundreds of thousands of visitors from all over the world every year. Scientists believe that it was created by volcanic activity around 60 million years ago, but legend has it that it was built to serve as a bridge by giant Finn McCool, so that he could go to meet his Scottish rival, Benandonner, for battle!

Bright lights: A view of the Europa hotel, one of the most famous hotels in Northern Ireland stands to the right of the picture. Over the years the hotel, the most bombed in Europe, has become emblematic of the resilient spirit of the people of Northern Ireland.

The future's bright: Belfast's Waterfront Hall, which opened in 1997, symbolized a new era of optimism and determination for the people of Northern Ireland. This magnificent £32 million dome, just five minutes drive from GBBCA, was chosen as Europe's Premier International Conference Centre in 2002 and is famed for its night-time illusion of appearing to float on the river Lagan.

Walls of Derry: children play on the 17th century battlements on the city walls of Londonderry, the only intact medieval walled city in Great Britain or Ireland, and one of the best preserved in Europe. The city endured one of the worst sieges history had ever seen in 1688, when those barricaded inside the walls were so hungry that they famously dined on dogs and rats! Nowadays the walls are a key tourist attraction.

Bella vista: This picturesque place is the world-renowned Royal County Down golf course, which has been used for over one hundred years. The course attracts many tourists each year, many of whom fly into GBBCA, from where it is a relatively short onward journey to their destination. The location of the course in Newcastle is perhaps best described in the famous song by Percy French: 'Where the Mountains of Mourne sweep down to the sea.'

Wheel of fortune: The Belfast Big Wheel arrived in the city in March 2007 and was an instant hit with residents and tourists who enjoyed a bird's eye view across the city. In the short space of time it has been here it has become one of Belfast's most recognisable landmarks.

Silver Streak

"GBBCA provides the ideal base for our operations. The airport has a unique position supporting Northern Ireland's economy and we believe that along with the range of services Flybe operates, we have formed a partnership which makes a significant contribution to Northern Ireland plc."

Andrea Hayes, Flybe General Manager of Market Development

GBBCA is proud to be 'The Home of Flybe', and it is not surprising given the long and mutually beneficial relationship between the airport and the airline. In 1983 Flybe was known as Spacegrand Aviation and had a strong reputation as an airline for the business commuter. Owned by the Walker Steel Group, it was one of the two airlines that initiated commercial flights from GBBCA. In 1985, Walker Steel amalgamated its Spacegrand and Jersey European brands, using the latter name until 2002, when it became Flybe.

Back in 1983, Spacegrand had seen great potential in extending its route network to Belfast and in purchasing aircraft from Shorts. Focusing on a target passenger proved hugely successful and the airport's numbers rose steadily, climbing from 85,000 in 1983 to 1.2 million in 1990. The pivotal role that the airline played in the airport's beginnings was the start of a long and fruitful association of mutual benefit that shows no signs of slowing down.

In the 90s, Jersey European became the first domestic airline in the UK to offer two classes when they launched their Business Class Service. 1993 was a stellar year for the airline, when it introduced the famous 146 Whisper Jets, renowned for their quietness. This was also the year that Flybe won the Best UK Regional Award, which it did again in 1994.

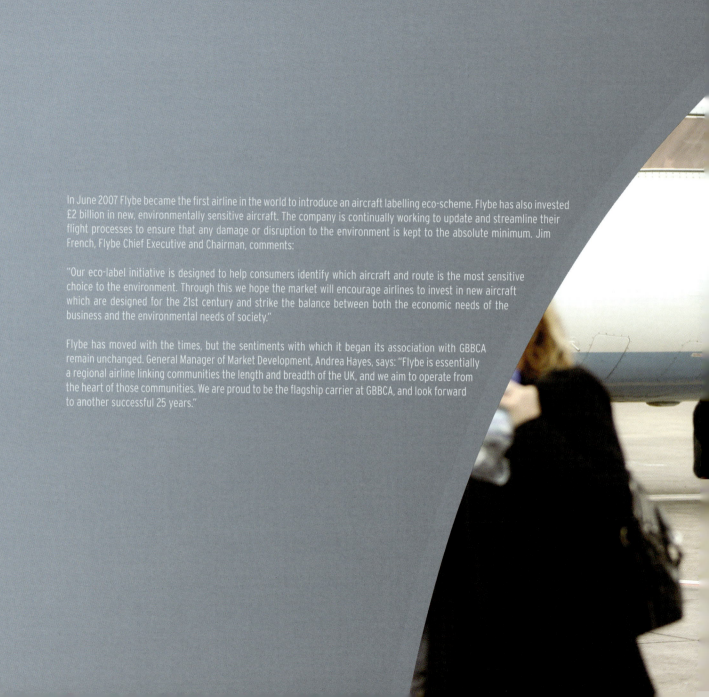

In June 2007 Flybe became the first airline in the world to introduce an aircraft labelling eco-scheme. Flybe has also invested £2 billion in new, environmentally sensitive aircraft. The company is continually working to update and streamline their flight processes to ensure that any damage or disruption to the environment is kept to the absolute minimum. Jim French, Flybe Chief Executive and Chairman, comments:

"Our eco-label initiative is designed to help consumers identify which aircraft and route is the most sensitive choice to the environment. Through this we hope the market will encourage airlines to invest in new aircraft which are designed for the 21st century and strike the balance between both the economic needs of the business and the environmental needs of society."

Flybe has moved with the times, but the sentiments with which it began its association with GBBCA remain unchanged. General Manager of Market Development, Andrea Hayes, says: "Flybe is essentially a regional airline linking communities the length and breadth of the UK, and we aim to operate from the heart of those communities. We are proud to be the flagship carrier at GBBCA, and look forward to another successful 25 years."

New arrival: GBGMD was the first aircraft to land at GBBCA on Monday, 7th February 1983, thus making it the aircraft to officially open the airport. The Spacegrand SGA 101 arrived from Blackpool at 08.25 and departed at 08.55 as the SGA 102 to the Isle of Man.

Bound for Blackpool: This De Havilland Twin Otter, pictured outside the airport's terminal, was the first aircraft to depart from GBBCA when it opened for commercial operations. The De Havilland flew the Belfast to Blackpool route twice a week.

Flying colours: Three Jersey European planes on the runway at GBBCA. The aircrafts are branded with the distinctive brightly-coloured Jersey European Airways logo, introduced in 1992. The two planes on the right are Shorts 360s. On the left is the F27 Fokker Friendship.

Bound for Old Trafford: school students set off to perform a special dance routine to commemorate the second anniversary of George Best's passing at the Trafford Centre in 2007. Pictured wishing them luck are Best's sister and her husband, Barbara and Norman McNarry, the Lord Mayor of Belfast, Chairperson of BELB Jim Rodgers, and Flybe's Andrea Hayes.

An eco first: Environment Minister Arlene Foster, examines Flybe's new eco-labelling system with Niall Duffy, Head of PR, and Andrea Hayes, General Manager. Flybe is the first airline in the world to use this system, which was introduced on 4th June 2007. The label shows a full range of environmental indicators per aircraft.

New targets: Miss Northern Ireland Catherine Milligan, aka Robin Hood, launches the new Flybe service from GBBCA to Robin Hood Doncaster/Sheffield with a flourish.

Surf's up: John McCurry, Irish Longboard Champion, pictured with Jenny Curran and Hayley McDonald, gets ready for Flybe's new service from GBBCA to Newquay. Newquay is regarded as the surf capital of the south coast of England.

It's a cracker!: Staff re-create Frank Carson's famous catchphrase as they launch the new flight route to Inverness. Inverness became a popular destination for those seeking Nessie!

Life and soul: Passengers enjoy a colourful welcome to Belfast, with dancers celebrating the launch of the new Brazil-manufactured Embraer 195 jet aircraft. The new millennium saw Flybe, by then UK's third largest scheduled airline, introduce many new flight routes.

It's a fine life: BBC1's I'd Do Anything star Samantha Barks, from the Isle of Man, makes a flying visit to Belfast courtesy of Flybe to celebrate her friend and fellow contestant Niamh Perry's 18th birthday. Flybe provided free weekly travel for Samantha's family throughout the show to ensure that they had ringside seats to cheer her on!

Golden Future

"We've come a long way in 25 years...We continue to plan for the future, with our considerable infrastructure investments and continue to meet the demand of travellers that Belfast, as a relatively new destination on the tourist trail, will continue to attract. With Northern Ireland experiencing renewed economic prosperity and many tourists visiting the region for the first time, we look forward to providing a service to our growing customer base."

Brian Ambrose, Chief Executive GBBCA

GBBCA's impressive 25-year rise from a Nissen hut to multi-million pound award-winning enterprise is down to its unique combination of grit, expertise and vision. One of the secrets of its success is its continual and unrelenting quest for a great airport experience. New owners ABN AMRO plan to continue this tradition on a larger scale than ever before. They have committed to a significant capital investment programme over the next five years to enhance customer provisions and facilities. These exciting new developments will include a new on-site hotel, new radar, a runway extension, and revised accommodation for airline engineering. The interior of the terminal will be reconfigured to provide an additional 60% retail space.

Projected figures for the future are also looking impressive. A 20% increase in passenger numbers is predicted for 2008. On average just under 50% of people arriving into GBBCA are visitors and new routes will further boost tourism and ensure that GBBCA continues to play a key role in developing Northern Ireland's economy. Employment at the airport is expected to grow to over 2,500 ensuring that GBBCA remains one of east Belfast's main employers.

GBBCA also prides itself on engaging with the community at a grass roots level. It appreciates that local residents are interested in the impact the airport has on their lives and will continue to do its utmost to maintain an open line of communication at all times. The airport's Corporate Social Responsibility (CSR) policy has led to numerous accolades and awards. The CSR plan for the future focuses primarily on local education and community funding, as Michelle Hatfield, Head of HR and Corporate Social Responsibility explains:

"We are very proud of our CSR programme. Over the next 25 years we want to build upon the existing strong relationship we have with the community and local schools. Gaining a greater understanding of local needs, investing in the future of our young people and employing local people is vital in shaping the future of not just the airport, but also the community in which it operates."

These are exciting times for Northern Ireland. No longer one of the best-kept secrets of Europe, Northern Ireland has rapidly become a tourist hot spot and Belfast's popularity is on the rise. GBBCA has been instrumental in this by providing visitors with a direct service to the very heart of the city.

"The airport is representative of how the city has risen and prospered over the last 25 years, despite its troubled past," say Brian Ambrose. "If one small airstrip, a Nissen hut and a handful of determined people can achieve all this in just 25 years, the opportunities abound for those who wish to grasp them."

Facts & Figures

- GBBCA was sold to ABN AMRO Global Infrastructure Fund for £132.5 million.
- GBBCA is three kilometres from Belfast City Centre.
- It is just 90 minutes away from anywhere in Northern Ireland.
- 2.2 million passengers used the airport in 2007.
- Approximately 7,000 passengers use the airport every day.
- Airside standards use nine bird calls to control bird activity on the runway.
- 16 runway inspections are carried out per day.
- 1000 employee hours are annually dedicated to working with the community.
- There are 20 check-in counters, 2 business lounges and 10 boarding gates.